Sketches and Songs

Kristi Casey

Presentation by *BookLeaf Publishing*

Web: www.bookleafpub.com

E-mail: info@bookleafpub.com

ISBN: 9789395950541

First edition 2023

Patience.
Know what you control.
Let everything else go.
3 September 2022 - Roswell, Georgia

Wild Season

Dam the river of my heart?

Might as well ask I stop breathing.

Holding back either would
break me.

You laugh.

I
fight
against
the
current.

This is no joke.

My back is arched
and silver.

I ride a savage desire,
an urge I've born
since birth.

I will
merge,
lose,
find,
and heal
my self.

Again.

This will be with
or without
you.

There must be,
and so there was,
a path through the darkness.
25 August 2022
Lethbridge Canada

Fear

You can't understand, she says,
Hope has never been kicked out of you.

That hurt runs so deep,
I see no way to cross it.
So I hold my tongue
as we race over the hills.

That night in London,
body booted and broken,
doll parts twisted and soaking
in garbage water.
No tears can reclaim what was taken
from you.

I imagine
the stinging realization:
no one is coming.
How you packed
all the stuffing
back in and patched
your self up.

The seams are close to bursting.
I want to open up the rage-sealed holes,

and re-set the hurt
so it can heal.

The scars cripple
and comfort
you.

Who am I to strip off that protective layer?
London is a million miles and years ago.
Though its lessons smell fresh
in the heat of this morning's disappointment.

Instead, I simply say, You're not stupid.
and hope you hear the river
underneath the words.

Please Don't Talk to Me

You are a picture in my head,
a perfect book I've read.
I'll love you till I'm dead,
but please don't talk to me.

You're a smile that always shines,
a friend who wines and dines,
a person so divine,
so please don't talk to me.

You are the love I've waited for,
the one I adore.
How could I want you more?
But please, don't talk to me.

You are the dream I've dared to dream,
my love supreme,
the coffee to my cream,
so please don't talk to me.

For, if I let you in,
And let my body grin,
My heart knows it will end.
I'd rather not begin.
I want to keep you at a distance-

only smiles and glimpses,
So please, please, please don't talk to me.

Obsessed

You don't sleep.
You say you never dream.
But does your mind wander?
Over my body, perhaps?

I hope so.

You live in my thoughts
so vividly
you are a part of me.

I cannot close my eyes
without feeling your lips on mine.
The way I feel . . .
I forget that it's not real.

Your truth is yours, no one else's. Live your truth, not theirs.
1 September 2022
Olalla, BC

Sweet Friend

Sweet friend,
when will you come by again?
I miss the way I feel when you smile.

Sweet friend,
when are you coming by again?
I need to be seen for a while.

I'm forgetting
and slipping away
slip slipping away
from myself
but maybe I
can be something you want?
Who would you like me to be?

Sweet friend,
when will you be back again?
Without your laugh, I feel so alone.

Sweet friend,
will I ever see you again?
I feel restless in this home.

I'm forgetting
and letting
myself
slip
away.

There is no beginning or end

September 2022
Powell River, British
Columbia, Canada

We just
go on.

As we must
With joy, wonder
and gratitude

The Prime

I know words
but I'm not bad at math.
I know
the numbers don't add up.

You want to carry
the one.
But it's a prime number.
It cannot be halved.
I know.
I've tried
to diminish
it,
cut it
down to
size
so it could fit in,
could be paired
up.

Alas-
it will not be told.
This stubborn heart of mine
always keeps
going

growing back
getting stronger.

What is mine
will stay
What will
will be replaced by
IS NOT
SOMETHING BETTER

Wild Winds Blow

Don't run from anguish,
don't hide for fear,
have the courage to face it:
promise me, dear.

Learn from the pain
don't let it cut twice.
From this grows wisdom:
head my advice.

Your skin will blister,
your heart will weep,
but trust me darling,
and you I'll keep.

The flames grow higher,
we are enmeshed.
Although I roam,
I love you best.

Lean into the sorrow,
let the tears flow.
I will shelter you
when the wild winds blow.

So Easy

I'm so easy
to fall in love with,
but I must be hard
to love.
I'm so easy to fall in love with.
Why am I hard to love?

I've got wit and sparkle aplenty.
I'm a fantastic host.
But if I shed a single tear,
my beau becomes a ghost.

I've got brains and charm for days,
and humor people adore,
but if I reveal my strengths,
lovers run for the door.

I'm a passionate volcano,
a goddess in hiking boots,
but when I mention attachment,
all I get are cool looks.

At night I dream about them . . .
the one or many who

will love my ragged pieces
and stick to me like glue.

I'm so easy
to fall in love with.
Why am I so hard
to love?
I'm so easy to fall in love with.
One day, I'll be easy to love.

Sometimes....
there are no
WORDS
4 September 2022
Roswell, Georgia

The Worm

I want to worm in through your eye hole,
squeeze everything else out,
so that the only thought
in your head
is me

me

me

me

me

Shed everything
that no longer
serves you!
Whistler, BC, Canada - 28 August 2022

The Problem

I know what you want.
Sorry to gin up the works.
You get what you get.

Maybe the problem isn't
with you or me, but with us.

Sorry People

It's no accident
that I found you sitting here,
pretending to care
about the whole world and all
the sorry people in it.

Asshole

She doesn't warn you.
She doesn't feel the need to
tilt her hand that way.

So don't expect her to bark.
Just don't be a damn asshole.

You
need
only
tilt
to
steer.
27 August 2022
Vancouver
British
Columbia
Canada

Flight Risk

If I bind you down,
to everything you promised,
would you still take flight
as soon as I let you go?
That's a risk I have to take.

The Making

I sharpen the blade.
I measure twice, make the mark,
and then guide the cut.
Somehow, I still have so much
more than I need. Is that bad?

Always be Snuggling.
30 August 2022
Olalla, B.C., Canada

Memory Fruit

Her feet jump water.
The trail — a ribbon of foam
and rainbow behind.
These lazy days, while bees buzz,
I eat memory fruit, and dream.

The Haunted

A bump on the stairs,
a creak from an empty room,
a door that closes
on its own. These things will spook
and scare us, but only once.

Clear out
the gunk.
Uproot
what's
dead.
Make
room
for
new
life.
21 August 2022 - Olalla

An Ode

Hail to thee, elders.
We never listened to you,
and still, we survived.

But how wise you really were.
From a distance, it's so clear.

It's not about avoiding pain, it's learning how to alchemize its wisdom and learning how to keep growing.
10 September 2022
Roswell, Georgia

Resolve

My resolve is strong.
I know this because you called,
and I let it ring,
ring, ring, ring, ring, ring, ring, ring,
and felt no remorse at all.

You don't always have
to be drowning...
29 August 2022
Olalla, British
Columbia, Canada

Autumn

Walking through the woods,
I see all colors sucked up
and spat out as leaves.
I hold dormant beauty in,
as they do and wait, and wait.

New Beginnings

I don't think of you.
I remember you daily.
Somehow, both are true.
I am not your enemy.
I am the one who used to …

Dousing does not cause you
to miss life, it helps you
enjoy it more....
26 August 2020
Vancouver
CANADA

Doubt Not

The night is so cold.
The days are growing shorter.
But your light still burns.
Doubt not that you are worthy.
Doubt those who insist you're not.

Let nature
take its time.
Savor it all.
22 September 2022
Sutee Naccache
44